MznLnx

Missing Links Exam Preps

Exam Prep for

Management Skills for Everyday Life: The Practical Coach

Caproni, 2nd Edition

The MznLnx Exam Prep is your link from the texbook and lecture to your exams.
The MznLnx Exam Preps are unauthorized and comprehensive reviews of your textbooks.

All material provided by MznLnx and Rico Publications (c) 2010
Textbook publishers and textbook authors do not particpate in or contribute to these reviews.

MznLnx

Rico
Publications

Exam Prep for Management Skills for Everyday Life: The Practical Coach
2nd Edition
Caproni

Publisher: Raymond Houge	*Product Manager:* Dave Mason
Assistant Editor: Michael Rouger	*Editorial Assitant:* Rachel Guzmanji
Text and Cover Designer: Lisa Buckner	*Pedagogy:* Debra Long
Marketing Manager: Sara Swagger	*Cover Image:* Jim Reed/Getty Images
Project Manager, Editorial Production: Jerry Emerson	*Text and Cover Printer:* City Printing, Inc.
Art Director: Vernon Lowerui	*Compositor:* Media Mix, Inc.

(c) 2010 Rico Publications

ALL RIGHTS RESERVED. No part of this work covered by the copyright may be reproduced or used in any form or by an means--graphic, electronic, or mechanical, including photocopying, recording, taping, Web distribution, information storage, and retrieval systems, or in any other manner--without the written permission of the publisher.

Printed in the United States
ISBN:

For more information about our products, contact us at:
Dave.Mason@RicoPublications.com

For permission to use material from this text or product, submit a request online to:
Dave.Mason@RicoPublications.com

Contents

CHAPTER 1
What Predicts Success? 1

CHAPTER 2
Developing Self-Awareness 7

CHAPTER 3
Building Trust 12

CHAPTER 4
Communicating Effectively 16

CHAPTER 5
Gaining and Using Sustainable, Ethical Power and Influence 21

CHAPTER 6
Managing Relationships with Your Bosses, Subordinates, and Peers 26

CHAPTER 7
Managing Cultural Diversity 34

CHAPTER 8
Creating High-Performing Teams 43

CHAPTER 9
Diverse Teams and Virtual Teams: Managing Differences and Distances 48

CHAPTER 10
Crafting a Life 53

ANSWER KEY 58

TO THE STUDENT

COMPREHENSIVE

The *MznLnx* Exam Prep series is designed to help you pass your exams. Editors at MznLnx review your textbooks and then prepare these practice exams to help you master the textbook material. Unlike study guides, workbooks, and practice tests provided by the texbook publisher and textbook authors, *MznLnx* gives you **all** of the material in each chapter in exam form, not just samples, so you can be sure to nail your exam.

MECHANICAL

The MznLnx Exam Prep series creates exams that will help you learn the subject matter as well as test you on your understanding. Each question is designed to help you master the concept. Just working through the exams, you gain an understanding of the subject--its a simple mechanical process that produces success.

INTEGRATED STUDY GUIDE AND REVIEW

MznLnx is not just a set of exams designed to test you, its also a comprehensive review of the subject content. Each exam question is also a review of the concept, making sure that you will get the answer correct without having to go to other sources of material. You learn as you go! Its the easiest way to pass an exam.

HUMOR

Studying can be tedious and dry. MznLnx's instructional design includes moderate humor within the exam questions on occassion, to break the tedium and revitalize the brain

Chapter 1. What Predicts Success?

1. The 'business case for _____', theorizes that in a global marketplace, a company that employs a diverse workforce (both men and women, people of many generations, people from ethnically and racially diverse backgrounds etc.) is better able to understand the demographics of the marketplace it serves and is thus better equipped to thrive in that marketplace than a company that has a more limited range of employee demographics.

   An additional corollary suggests that a company that supports the _____ of its workforce can also improve employee satisfaction, productivity and retention.

   a. Trademark
   b. Virtual team
   c. Diversity
   d. Kanban

2. _____ in its literal sense is the process of transformation of local or regional phenomena into global ones. It can be described as a process by which the people of the world are unified into a single society and function together.

   This process is a combination of economic, technological, sociocultural and political forces.

   a. Collaborative Planning, Forecasting and Replenishment
   b. Globalization
   c. Histogram
   d. Cost Management

3. The _____ captures an expanded spectrum of values and criteria for measuring organizational success: economic, ecological and social. With the ratification of the United Nations and ICLEI _____ standard for urban and community accounting in early 2007, this became the dominant approach to public sector full cost accounting. Similar UN standards apply to natural capital and human capital measurement to assist in measurements required by _____, e.g. the ecoBudget standard for reporting ecological footprint.
   a. 28-hour day
   b. 33 Strategies of War
   c. 1990 Clean Air Act
   d. Triple bottom line

4. The term '_____' refers to the concept of collecting information and attempting to spot a pattern in the information. In some fields of study, the term '_____' has more formally-defined meanings.

   In project management _____ is a mathematical technique that uses historical results to predict future outcome.

a. Least squares
b. Regression analysis
c. Stepwise regression
d. Trend analysis

5. _____-model (SCOR(r)) is a process reference model developed by the management consulting firm PRTM and AMR Research and endorsed by the Supply-Chain Council (SCC) as the cross-industry de facto standard diagnostic tool for supply chain management. SCOR enables users to address, improve, and communicate supply chain management practices within and between all interested parties in the Extended Enterprise.

SCOR(r) is a management tool, spanning from the supplier's supplier to the customer's customer. The model has been developed by the members of the Council on a volunteer basis to describe the business activities associated with all phases of satisfying a customer's demand.

a. Delayed differentiation
b. Supply Chain Risk Management
c. Supply chain management software
d. Supply-Chain Operations Reference

6. _____ , often measured as an _____ Quotient (EQ), is a term that describes the ability, capacity, skill or (in the case of the trait _____ model) a self-perceived ability, to identify, assess, and manage the emotions of one's self, of others, and of groups. Different models have been proposed for the definition of _____ and disagreement exists as to how the term should be used. Despite these disagreements, which are often highly technical, the ability _____ and trait _____ models (but not the mixed models) are enjoying considerable support in the literature and have successful applications in many different domains.
a. AAAI
b. A4e
c. A Stake in the Outcome
d. Emotional intelligence

7. _____ describes the situation when output from (or information about the result of) an event or phenomenon in the past will influence the same event/phenomenon in the present or future. When an event is part of a chain of cause-and-effect that forms a circuit or loop, then the event is said to 'feed back' into itself.

_____ is also a synonym for:

- _____ signal; the information about the initial event that is the basis for subsequent modification of the event.
- _____ loop; the causal path that leads from the initial generation of the _____ signal to the subsequent modification of the event.

_____ is a mechanism, process or signal that is looped back to control a system within itself. Such a loop is called a _____ loop.

a. Feedback loop
b. Positive feedback
c. 1990 Clean Air Act
d. Feedback

8. _____ is purposeful and reflective judgment about what to believe or what to do in response to observations, experience, verbal or written expressions, or arguments. _____ might involve determining the meaning and significance of what is observed or expressed, or, concerning a given inference or argument, determining whether there is adequate justification to accept the conclusion as true. Hence, Fisher ' Scriven define _____ as 'Skilled, active, interpretation and evaluation of observations, communications, information, and argumentation.' Parker ' Moore define it more narrowly as the careful, deliberate determination of whether one should accept, reject, or suspend judgment about a claim and the degree of confidence with which one accepts or rejects it.
   a. Virtual team
   b. Risk management
   c. Kanban
   d. Critical thinking

9. A _____ is a contemporary apporach to organizational design. It is an organization that is not defined by, or limited to, the horizontal, vertical, or external boundaries imposed by a predefined structure. This term was coined by former GE chairman Jack Welch because he wanted to eliminate vertical and horizontal boundaries within GE and break down external barriers between the company and its customers and suppliers.
   a. Headquarters
   b. Business Roundtable
   c. Chief risk officer
   d. Boundaryless organization

10. _____ refers to increasing the spiritual, political, social or economic strength of individuals and communities. It often involves the empowered developing confidence in their own capacities.

The term Human _____ covers a vast landscape of meanings, interpretations, definitions and disciplines ranging from psychology and philosophy to the highly commercialized Self-Help industry and Motivational sciences.

   a. A4e
   b. AAAI
   c. A Stake in the Outcome
   d. Empowerment

11. A _____ in today's workforce is an individual that is valued for their ability to interpret information within a specific subject area. They will often advance the overall understanding of that subject through focused analysis, design and/or development. They use research skills to define problems and to identify alternatives.
   a. Career development
   b. Customer satisfaction
   c. Business rule
   d. Knowledge worker

12. _____ is a pedagogical concept according to which newly acquired skills should be practiced well beyond the point of initial mastery, leading to automaticity.

The Yerkes-Dodson law predicts that _____ can improve performance in states of high arousal.

   a. AAAI
   b. A4e
   c. A Stake in the Outcome
   d. Overlearning

13. The _____ is the labour pool in employment. It is generally used to describe those working for a single company or industry, but can also apply to a geographic region like a city, country, state, etc. The term generally excludes the employers or management, and implies those involved in manual labour.
   a. Work-life balance
   b. Division of labour
   c. Pink-collar worker
   d. Workforce

14. _____ is the 'lifelong, lifewide, voluntary, and self-motivated' pursuit of knowledge for either personal or professional reasons. As such, it not only enhances social inclusion, active citizenship and personal development, but also competitiveness and employability.

The term recognises that learning is not confined to childhood or the classroom, but takes place throughout life and in a range of situations.

   a. Lifelong Learning
   b. 33 Strategies of War
   c. 1990 Clean Air Act
   d. 28-hour day

15. _____ is a term used to describe any moral, political that stresses human interdependence and the importance of a collective, rather than the importance of separate individuals. Collectivists focus on community and society, and seek to give priority to group goals over individual goals. The philosophical underpinnings of _____ are for some related to holism or organicism - the view that the whole is greater than the sum of its parts/pieces.
   a. 1990 Clean Air Act
   b. Collectivism
   c. Collaborative methods
   d. 28-hour day

16. _____ is 'interfirm coordination that is characterized by organic or informal social systems, in contrast to bureaucratic structures within firms and formal contractual relationships between them.(Gerlach, 1992:64; Nohria, 1992)' A useful survey of network organization theory appears in Van Alstyne (1997).

The concepts of privatization, public private partnership, and contracting are defined in this context.

As a concept, _____ explains increased efficiency and reduced agency problems for organizations existing in highly turbulent environments . Due to the rapid pace of modern society and competitive pressures from globalization, _____ has gained prominence and development among sociological theorists. As a concept, _____ explains increased efficiency and reduced agency problems for organizations existing in highly turbulent environments.

   a. 1990 Clean Air Act
   b. 28-hour day
   c. 33 Strategies of War
   d. Network governance

17. An _____ is a mostly hierarchical concept of subordination of entities that collaborate and contribute to serve one common aim.

Organizations are a variant of clustered entities. The structure of an organization is usually set up in many a styles, dependent on their objectives and ambience.

a. Organizational development
b. Informal organization
c. Organizational structure
d. Open shop

18. _____ is the process of dispersing decision-making governance closer to the people or citizen. It includes the dispersal of administration or governance in sectors or areas like engineering, management science, political science, political economy, sociology and economics. _____ is also possible in the dispersal of population and employment.
a. Decentralization
b. Frenemy
c. Formula for Change
d. Business plan

Chapter 2. Developing Self-Awareness

1. A _____ is a name or trademark connected with a product or producer. _____s have become increasingly important components of culture and the economy, now being described as 'cultural accessories and personal philosophies'.

    Some people distinguish the psychological aspect of a _____ from the experiential aspect.

    a. Brand loyalty
    b. Brand extension
    c. Brand awareness
    d. Brand

2. In psychology, _____ reflects a person's overall evaluation or appraisal of his or her own worth.

    _____ encompasses beliefs (for example, 'I am competent/incompetent') and emotions (for example, triumph/despair, pride/shame.) Behavior may reflect _____

    a. 28-hour day
    b. 1990 Clean Air Act
    c. 33 Strategies of War
    d. Self-esteem

3. In economics, business, retail, and accounting, a _____ is the value of money that has been used up to produce something, and hence is not available for use anymore. In economics, a _____ is an alternative that is given up as a result of a decision. In business, the _____ may be one of acquisition, in which case the amount of money expended to acquire it is counted as _____.

    a. Fixed costs
    b. Cost allocation
    c. Cost overrun
    d. Cost

4. In mathematics, _____ is used to refer to various properties meaning, in some sense, 'all one piece'. When a mathematical object has such a property, we say it is connected; otherwise it is disconnected. When a disconnected object can be split naturally into connected pieces, each piece is usually called a component (or connected component.)

    a. Connectedness
    b. 28-hour day
    c. 33 Strategies of War
    d. 1990 Clean Air Act

Chapter 2. Developing Self-Awareness

5. _____ is a concept from the field of social psychology that is commonly used to describe the predisposition that individuals have 'to distort self-appraisals so as to maintain the most favorable self-view'. _____ involves sustaining and augmenting a positive view of the self; specifically, people are likely to over-emphasize favorable evaluations of themselves, while they are inclined to minimize or forget critical assessments of themselves. In addition, the concept of _____ suggests that people tend to look for flattering evaluations from others concerning their achievements and talents.

   a. Social loafing
   b. Machiavellianism
   c. Persuasion
   d. Self-enhancement

6. _____ is the self-government of a nation, country or some portion thereof, generally exercising sovereignty.

The term _____ is used in contrast to subjugation, which refers to a region as a 'territory' --subject to the political and military control of an external government. The word is sometimes used in a weaker sense to contrast with hegemony, the indirect control of one nation by another, more powerful nation.

   a. Independence
   b. A Stake in the Outcome
   c. A4e
   d. AAAI

7. The 'business case for _____', theorizes that in a global marketplace, a company that employs a diverse workforce (both men and women, people of many generations, people from ethnically and racially diverse backgrounds etc.) is better able to understand the demographics of the marketplace it serves and is thus better equipped to thrive in that marketplace than a company that has a more limited range of employee demographics.

An additional corollary suggests that a company that supports the _____ of its workforce can also improve employee satisfaction, productivity and retention.

   a. Diversity
   b. Kanban
   c. Trademark
   d. Virtual team

8. _____ is a dynamic of being mutually and physically responsible to and sharing a common set of principles with others. This concept differs distinctly from 'dependence' in that an interdependent relationship implies that all participants are emotionally, economically, ecologically and or morally 'interdependent.' Some people advocate freedom or independence as a sort of ultimate good; others do the same with devotion to one's family, community, or society. _____ recognizes the truth in each position and weaves them together.

a. A4e
b. A Stake in the Outcome
c. AAAI
d. Interdependence

9. _____ refers to increasing the spiritual, political, social or economic strength of individuals and communities. It often involves the empowered developing confidence in their own capacities.

The term Human _____ covers a vast landscape of meanings, interpretations, definitions and disciplines ranging from psychology and philosophy to the highly commercialized Self-Help industry and Motivational sciences.

   a. A Stake in the Outcome
   b. A4e
   c. AAAI
   d. Empowerment

10. _____ occurs when an individual's thoughts or actions are affected by other people. _____ takes many forms and can be seen in conformity, socialization, peer pressure, obedience, leadership, persuasion, sales, and marketing. Harvard psychologist, Herbert Kelman identified three broad varieties of _____.
   a. Soft skill
   b. Social awareness
   c. Role conflict
   d. Social influence

11. The _____ captures an expanded spectrum of values and criteria for measuring organizational success: economic, ecological and social. With the ratification of the United Nations and ICLEI _____ standard for urban and community accounting in early 2007, this became the dominant approach to public sector full cost accounting. Similar UN standards apply to natural capital and human capital measurement to assist in measurements required by _____, e.g. the ecoBudget standard for reporting ecological footprint.
   a. Triple bottom line
   b. 33 Strategies of War
   c. 1990 Clean Air Act
   d. 28-hour day

12. _____ is, according to the OED, 'the employment of cunning and duplicity in statecraft or in general conduct', deriving from the Italian Renaissance diplomat and writer Niccolò Machiavelli, who wrote Il Principe and other works. Machiavellian and variants became very popular in the late 16th century in English, though '_____' itself is first cited by the OED from 1626. The word has a similar use in modern psychology.
   a. Self-enhancement
   b. Persuasion
   c. Personal space
   d. Machiavellianism

13. _____ can be regarded as an outcome of mental processes (cognitive process) leading to the selection of a course of action among several alternatives. Every _____ process produces a final choice. The output can be an action or an opinion of choice.
   a. 33 Strategies of War
   b. 1990 Clean Air Act
   c. Decision making
   d. 28-hour day

14. _____ is the belief that one is capable of performing in a certain manner to attain certain goals. It is a belief that one has the capabilities to execute the courses of actions required to manage prospective situations. Unlike efficacy, which is the power to produce an effect (in essence, competence), _____ is the belief (whether or not accurate) that one has the power to produce that effect.
   a. 28-hour day
   b. Self-efficacy
   c. 33 Strategies of War
   d. 1990 Clean Air Act

15. _____ is the use of marginal concepts within economics. (Marginal concepts are associated with a specific change in the quantity used of a good or of a service, as opposed to some notion of the over-all significance of that class of good or service, or of some total quantity thereof.) The central concept of _____ proper is that of marginal utility, but marginalists following the lead of Alfred Marshall were further heavily dependent upon the concept of marginal physical productivity in their explanation of cost; and the neoclassical tradition that emerged from British _____ generally abandoned the concept of utility and gave marginal rates of substitution a more fundamental rôle in analysis.
   a. 28-hour day
   b. 1990 Clean Air Act
   c. 33 Strategies of War
   d. Marginalism

16. The _____ arose out of the social and intellectual milieu of the 1960s and formed around the concept of cultivating extraordinary potential that its advocates believed to lie largely untapped in most people. The movement took as its premise the belief that through the development of 'human potential', humans can experience an exceptional quality of life filled with happiness, creativity, and fulfillment. As a corollary, those who begin to unleash this assumed potential often find themselves directing their actions within society towards assisting others to release their potential.
   a. 33 Strategies of War
   b. Human Potential Movement
   c. 1990 Clean Air Act
   d. 28-hour day

17. In attribution theory, the _____ is a theory describing cognitive tendency to predominantly over-value dispositional explanations for the observed behaviors of others, thus under-valuing or acknowledging the potentiality of situational attributions or situational explanations for the behavioral motives of others. In other words, people predominantly presume that the actions of others are indicative of the 'kind' of person they are, rather than the kind of situations that compels their behavior. However, the over attribution effect generally does not account for our own ability to self-justify our behaviors; we tend to prefer interpreting our own actions in terms of the situational variables accessible to our awareness.
   a. Confirmation bias
   b. Halo effect
   c. Pygmalion effect
   d. Fundamental attribution error

Chapter 3. Building Trust

1. The _____ captures an expanded spectrum of values and criteria for measuring organizational success: economic, ecological and social. With the ratification of the United Nations and ICLEI _____ standard for urban and community accounting in early 2007, this became the dominant approach to public sector full cost accounting. Similar UN standards apply to natural capital and human capital measurement to assist in measurements required by _____, e.g. the ecoBudget standard for reporting ecological footprint.
    a. Triple bottom line
    b. 33 Strategies of War
    c. 1990 Clean Air Act
    d. 28-hour day

2. In decision theory and estimation theory, the _____ of an estimator, $\hat{\theta}$, of an unknown parameter of the distribution, θ, is the expected value of the loss function

$$R(\theta, \hat{\theta}) = \mathbb{E}_\theta L(\theta, \hat{\theta}) = \int L(\theta, \hat{\theta}) \, dP_\theta.$$

where dP_θ is a probability measure parametrized by θ.

- For a scalar parameter θ and a quadratic loss function,

$$L(\theta, \hat{\theta}) = (\theta - \hat{\theta})^2$$

    the _____ function becomes the mean squared error of the estimate,

$$R(\theta, \hat{\theta}) = E_\theta (\theta - \hat{\theta})^2$$

- In density estimation, the unknown parameter is probability density itself. The loss function is typically chosen to be a norm in an appropriate function space. For example, for L^2 norm,

$$L(f, \hat{f}) = \|f - \hat{f}\|_2^2$$

    the _____ function becomes the mean integrated squared error

$$R(f, \hat{f}) = E\|f - \hat{f}\|^2$$

a. Financial modeling
b. Linear model
c. Risk
d. Risk aversion

3. _____ is one of the managerial functions like planning, organizing, staffing and directing. It is an important function because it helps to check the errors and to take the corrective action so that deviation from standards are minimized and stated goals of the organization are achieved in desired manner. According to modern concepts, _____ is a foreseeing action whereas earlier concept of _____ was used only when errors were detected. _____ in management means setting standards, measuring actual performance and taking corrective action.

   a. Schedule of reinforcement
   b. Decision tree pruning
   c. Turnover
   d. Control

4. An _____ is a mostly hierarchical concept of subordination of entities that collaborate and contribute to serve one common aim.

Organizations are a variant of clustered entities. The structure of an organization is usually set up in many a styles, dependent on their objectives and ambience.

   a. Organizational structure
   b. Organizational development
   c. Open shop
   d. Informal organization

5. _____ describes the situation when output from (or information about the result of) an event or phenomenon in the past will influence the same event/phenomenon in the present or future. When an event is part of a chain of cause-and-effect that forms a circuit or loop, then the event is said to 'feed back' into itself.

_____ is also a synonym for:

- _____ signal; the information about the initial event that is the basis for subsequent modification of the event.
- _____ loop; the causal path that leads from the initial generation of the _____ signal to the subsequent modification of the event.

_____ is a mechanism, process or signal that is looped back to control a system within itself. Such a loop is called a _____ loop.

a. Feedback loop
   b. 1990 Clean Air Act
   c. Positive feedback
   d. Feedback

6. _____ is the concept of how effective an organization is in achieving the outcomes the organization intends to produce. The idea of _____ is especially important for non-profit organizations as most people who donate money to non-profit organizations and charities are interested in knowing whether the organization is effective in accomplishing its goals.

An organization's effectiveness is also dependent on its communicative competence and ethics.

   a. Organizational development
   b. Informal organization
   c. Organizational structure
   d. Organizational effectiveness

7. The 'business case for _____', theorizes that in a global marketplace, a company that employs a diverse workforce (both men and women, people of many generations, people from ethnically and racially diverse backgrounds etc.) is better able to understand the demographics of the marketplace it serves and is thus better equipped to thrive in that marketplace than a company that has a more limited range of employee demographics.

An additional corollary suggests that a company that supports the _____ of its workforce can also improve employee satisfaction, productivity and retention.

   a. Trademark
   b. Kanban
   c. Virtual team
   d. Diversity

8. _____ is an approach to personal, organizational and cultural change based on the idea that every community or group of people performing a similar function has certain individuals (the 'Positive Deviants') whose special attitudes, practices/ strategies/ behaviors enable them to function more effectively than others with the exact same resources and conditions. Because Positive Deviants derive their extraordinary capabilities from the identical environmental conditions as those around them, but are not constrained by conventional wisdoms, Positive Deviants standards for attitudes, thinking and behavior are readily accepted as the foundation for profound organizational and cultural change.

For example, even though poverty is often the root-cause of ill health, in any community there will usually be some families, the Positive Deviants, that manage to stay healthy, or raise healthy kids, despite their poverty.

a. 33 Strategies of War
b. 1990 Clean Air Act
c. 28-hour day
d. Positive deviance

Chapter 4. Communicating Effectively

1. _____ has been described as the 'process of social influence in which one person can enlist the aid and support of others in the accomplishment of a common task'. A definition more inclusive of followers comes from Alan Keith of Genentech who said '_____ is ultimately about creating a way for people to contribute to making something extraordinary happen.'

   _____ is one of the most salient aspects of the organizational context. However, defining _____ has been challenging.

   a. Situational leadership
   b. 1990 Clean Air Act
   c. 28-hour day
   d. Leadership

2. _____ is a subfield of the larger discipline of communication studies. _____, as a field, is the consideration, analysis, and criticism of the role of communication in organizational contexts.

   The field traces its lineage through business information, business communication, and early mass communication studies published in the 1930s through the 1950s.

   a. A Stake in the Outcome
   b. AAAI
   c. A4e
   d. Organizational communication

3. _____ is a type of thought exhibited by group members who try to minimize conflict and reach consensus without critically testing, analyzing, and evaluating ideas. Individual creativity, uniqueness, and independent thinking are lost in the pursuit of group cohesiveness, as are the advantages of reasonable balance in choice and thought that might normally be obtained by making decisions as a group. During _____, members of the group avoid promoting viewpoints outside the comfort zone of consensus thinking.

   a. Self-report inventory
   b. Diffusion of responsibility
   c. Groupthink
   d. Psychological statistics

4. _____ is a term used in economics and game theory to describe an economic situation or game in which knowledge about other market participants or players is available to all participants. Every player knows the payoffs and strategies available to other players.

   _____ is one of the theoretical pre-conditions of an efficient perfectly competitive market.

a. Mixed strategy
b. Transferable utility
c. Global games
d. Complete information

5. _____, sometimes referred to as 'cumulative causation', is a feedback loop system in which the system responds to perturbation in the same direction as the perturbation. In contrast, a system that responds to the perturbation in the opposite direction is called a negative feedback system. These concepts were first recognized as broadly applicable by Norbert Wiener in his 1948 work on cybernetics.
   a. Negative feedback
   b. 1990 Clean Air Act
   c. Feedback loop
   d. Positive feedback

6. _____ describes the situation when output from (or information about the result of) an event or phenomenon in the past will influence the same event/phenomenon in the present or future. When an event is part of a chain of cause-and-effect that forms a circuit or loop, then the event is said to 'feed back' into itself.

   _____ is also a synonym for:

   - _____ signal; the information about the initial event that is the basis for subsequent modification of the event.
   - _____ loop; the causal path that leads from the initial generation of the _____ signal to the subsequent modification of the event.

   _____ is a mechanism, process or signal that is looped back to control a system within itself. Such a loop is called a _____ loop.

   a. Positive feedback
   b. Feedback loop
   c. 1990 Clean Air Act
   d. Feedback

7. In contrast, positive feedback is a feedback in which the system responds in the same direction as the perturbation, resulting in amplification of the original signal instead of stabilizing the signal. A positive feedback of 100% or greater will result in a runaway situation. Both positive and _____ require a feedback loop to operate.

Chapter 4. Communicating Effectively

   a. 1990 Clean Air Act
   b. Positive feedback
   c. Negative feedback
   d. Feedback loop

8. In the fields of science, engineering, industry and statistics, _____ is the degree of closeness of a measured or calculated quantity to its actual (true) value. _____ is closely related to precision, also called reproducibility or repeatability, the degree to which further measurements or calculations show the same or similar results. _____ indicates proximity to the true value, precision to the repeatability or reproducibility of the measurement

The results of calculations or a measurement can be accurate but not precise, precise but not accurate, neither, or both.

   a. A Stake in the Outcome
   b. A4e
   c. Accuracy
   d. AAAI

9. _____ is an organization's process of defining its strategy and making decisions on allocating its resources to pursue this strategy, including its capital and people. Various business analysis techniques can be used in _____, including SWOT analysis (Strengths, Weaknesses, Opportunities, and Threats) and PEST analysis (Political, Economic, Social, and Technological analysis) or STEER analysis involving Socio-cultural, Technological, Economic, Ecological, and Regulatory factors and EPISTEL (Environment, Political, Informatic, Social, Technological, Economic and Legal)

_____ is the formal consideration of an organization's future course. All _____ deals with at least one of three key questions:

   1. 'What do we do?'
   2. 'For whom do we do it?'
   3. 'How do we excel?'

In business _____, the third question is better phrased 'How can we beat or avoid competition?'. (Bradford and Duncan, page 1.)

   a. 1990 Clean Air Act
   b. 33 Strategies of War
   c. 28-hour day
   d. Strategic planning

10. _____ is one of the managerial functions like planning, organizing, staffing and directing. It is an important function because it helps to check the errors and to take the corrective action so that deviation from standards are minimized and stated goals of the organization are achieved in desired manner.According to modern concepts, _____ is a foreseeing action whereas earlier concept of _____ was used only when errors were detected. _____ in management means setting standards, measuring actual performance and taking corrective action.
   a. Control
   b. Turnover
   c. Schedule of reinforcement
   d. Decision tree pruning

11. The trait of _____ is a central dimension of human personality. Extraverts (also spelled extroverts) tend to be gregarious, assertive, and interested in seeking out excitement. Introverts, in contrast, tend to be more reserved, less outgoing, and less sociable.
   a. A4e
   b. Extraversion-introversion
   c. A Stake in the Outcome
   d. AAAI

12. _____ , was a German-born American anthropologist-linguist and a leader in American structural linguistics. He was one of the creators of what is now called the Sapir-Whorf hypothesis. He is arguably the most influential figure in American linguistics, influencing several generations of linguists across several schools of the discipline.
   a. Adam Smith
   b. Abraham Harold Maslow
   c. Affiliation
   d. Edward Sapir

13. _____ can be defined as the idea generation, concept development, testing and manufacturing or implementation of a physical object or service. _____ers conceptualize and evaluate ideas, making them tangible through products in a more systematic approach. The role of a _____er encompasses many characteristics of the marketing manager, product manager, industrial designer and design engineer.
   a. Adam Smith
   b. Product design
   c. Affiliation
   d. Abraham Harold Maslow

14. _____ is the change (processing) of information in any manner detectable by an observer. As such, it is a process which describes everything which happens (changes) in the universe, from the falling of a rock (a change in position) to the printing of a text file from a digital computer system. In the latter case, an information processor is changing the form of presentation of that text file.
   a. A Stake in the Outcome
   b. A4e
   c. AAAI
   d. Information processing

Chapter 5. Gaining and Using Sustainable, Ethical Power and Influence

1. _____ is a term that was popularized by renowned psychologist David McClelland in 1961. However, it should be recognized that McClellend's thinking was strongly influenced by the pioneering work of Henry Murray who first identified underlying psychological human needs and motivational processes (1938.) It was Murray who set out a taxonomy of needs, including Achievement, Power and Affiliation - and placed these in the context of an integrated motivational model.
   a. Two-factor theory
   b. Need for Power
   c. 1990 Clean Air Act
   d. Need for Achievement

2. _____ is a dynamic of being mutually and physically responsible to and sharing a common set of principles with others. This concept differs distinctly from 'dependence' in that an interdependent relationship implies that all participants are emotionally, economically, ecologically and or morally 'interdependent.' Some people advocate freedom or independence as a sort of ultimate good; others do the same with devotion to one's family, community, or society. _____ recognizes the truth in each position and weaves them together.
   a. A Stake in the Outcome
   b. AAAI
   c. Interdependence
   d. A4e

3. The _____ captures an expanded spectrum of values and criteria for measuring organizational success: economic, ecological and social. With the ratification of the United Nations and ICLEI _____ standard for urban and community accounting in early 2007, this became the dominant approach to public sector full cost accounting. Similar UN standards apply to natural capital and human capital measurement to assist in measurements required by _____, e.g. the ecoBudget standard for reporting ecological footprint.
   a. 33 Strategies of War
   b. 1990 Clean Air Act
   c. 28-hour day
   d. Triple bottom line

4. _____ is a form of communication that typically attempts to persuade potential customers to purchase or to consume more of a particular brand of product or service. 'While now central to the contemporary global economy and the reproduction of global production networks, it is only quite recently that _____ has been more than a marginal influence on patterns of sales and production. The formation of modern _____ was intimately bound up with the emergence of new forms of monopoly capitalism around the end of the 19th and beginning of the 20th century as one element in corporate strategies to create, organize and where possible control markets, especially for mass produced consumer goods.
   a. A Stake in the Outcome
   b. A4e
   c. Advertising
   d. AAAI

Chapter 5. Gaining and Using Sustainable, Ethical Power and Influence

5. _____ has been described as the 'process of social influence in which one person can enlist the aid and support of others in the accomplishment of a common task'. A definition more inclusive of followers comes from Alan Keith of Genentech who said '_____ is ultimately about creating a way for people to contribute to making something extraordinary happen.'

_____ is one of the most salient aspects of the organizational context. However, defining _____ has been challenging.

   a. Situational leadership
   b. 28-hour day
   c. 1990 Clean Air Act
   d. Leadership

6. _____ is a compliance tactic that involves getting a person to agree to a large request by first setting them up by having that person agree to a modest request.

In an early study, a team of psychologists telephoned housewives in California and asked if the women would answer a few questions about the household products they used. Three days later, the psychologists called again.

   a. 28-hour day
   b. 1990 Clean Air Act
   c. Foot-in-the-door technique
   d. 33 Strategies of War

7. _____ refers to increasing the spiritual, political, social or economic strength of individuals and communities. It often involves the empowered developing confidence in their own capacities.

The term Human _____ covers a vast landscape of meanings, interpretations, definitions and disciplines ranging from psychology and philosophy to the highly commercialized Self-Help industry and Motivational sciences.

   a. Empowerment
   b. A Stake in the Outcome
   c. AAAI
   d. A4e

8. _____ is the process of recruiting individuals to fill executive positions in organizations. _____ may be performed by an organization's board of directors, by executives in the organization, or by an outside _____ organization.

Chapter 5. Gaining and Using Sustainable, Ethical Power and Influence 23

The _____ profession has two distinct fields, retained _____ and contingency search.

a. Internet recruiting
b. Employee referral
c. Employment agency
d. Executive search

9. A _____ is a process in which a potential employee is evaluated by an employer for prospective employment in their company, organization and was established in the late 16th century.

A _____ typically precedes the hiring decision, and is used to evaluate the candidate. The interview is usually preceded by the evaluation of submitted résumés from interested candidates, then selecting a small number of candidates for interviews.

a. Payrolling
b. Job interview
c. Split shift
d. Supported employment

10. Within graph theory and network analysis, there are various measures of the _____ of a vertex within a graph that determine the relative importance of a vertex within the graph (for example, how important a person is within a social network, or, in the theory of space syntax, how important a room is within a building or how well-used a road is within an urban network.)

There are four measures of _____ that are widely used in network analysis: degree _____, betweenness, closeness, and eigenvector _____.

The first, and simplest, is degree _____.

a. 28-hour day
b. 33 Strategies of War
c. 1990 Clean Air Act
d. Centrality

11. A _____ is an alliance among individuals or groups, during which they cooperate in joint action, each in his own self-interest, joining forces together for a common cause. This alliance may be temporary or a matter of convenience. A _____ thus differs from a more formal covenant.

Chapter 5. Gaining and Using Sustainable, Ethical Power and Influence

a. Coalition
b. 1990 Clean Air Act
c. 33 Strategies of War
d. 28-hour day

12. In contrast, positive feedback is a feedback in which the system responds in the same direction as the perturbation, resulting in amplification of the original signal instead of stabilizing the signal. A positive feedback of 100% or greater will result in a runaway situation. Both positive and _____ require a feedback loop to operate.

a. Negative feedback
b. Positive feedback
c. Feedback loop
d. 1990 Clean Air Act

13. _____ describes the situation when output from (or information about the result of) an event or phenomenon in the past will influence the same event/phenomenon in the present or future. When an event is part of a chain of cause-and-effect that forms a circuit or loop, then the event is said to 'feed back' into itself.

_____ is also a synonym for:

- _____ signal; the information about the initial event that is the basis for subsequent modification of the event.
- _____ loop; the causal path that leads from the initial generation of the _____ signal to the subsequent modification of the event.

_____ is a mechanism, process or signal that is looped back to control a system within itself. Such a loop is called a _____ loop.

a. Feedback loop
b. Positive feedback
c. 1990 Clean Air Act
d. Feedback

14. _____ is purposeful and reflective judgment about what to believe or what to do in response to observations, experience, verbal or written expressions, or arguments. _____ might involve determining the meaning and significance of what is observed or expressed, or, concerning a given inference or argument, determining whether there is adequate justification to accept the conclusion as true. Hence, Fisher ' Scriven define _____ as 'Skilled, active, interpretation and evaluation of observations, communications, information, and argumentation.' Parker ' Moore define it more narrowly as the careful, deliberate determination of whether one should accept, reject, or suspend judgment about a claim and the degree of confidence with which one accepts or rejects it.

a. Critical thinking
b. Virtual team
c. Risk management
d. Kanban

15. _____ is a form of social influence. It is the process of guiding people and oneself toward the adoption of an idea, attitude, or action by rational and symbolic (though not always logical) means. It is strategy of problem-solving relying on 'appeals' rather than coercion.
a. Social loafing
b. Personal space
c. Self-enhancement
d. Persuasion

Chapter 6. Managing Relationships with Your Bosses, Subordinates, and Peers

1. An _____ is a mostly hierarchical concept of subordination of entities that collaborate and contribute to serve one common aim.

Organizations are a variant of clustered entities. The structure of an organization is usually set up in many a styles, dependent on their objectives and ambience.

   a. Organizational development
   b. Informal organization
   c. Open shop
   d. Organizational structure

2. _____ is a dynamic of being mutually and physically responsible to and sharing a common set of principles with others. This concept differs distinctly from 'dependence' in that an interdependent relationship implies that all participants are emotionally, economically, ecologically and or morally 'interdependent.' Some people advocate freedom or independence as a sort of ultimate good; others do the same with devotion to one's family, community, or society. _____ recognizes the truth in each position and weaves them together.
   a. AAAI
   b. A Stake in the Outcome
   c. A4e
   d. Interdependence

3. _____ has been described as the 'process of social influence in which one person can enlist the aid and support of others in the accomplishment of a common task' . A definition more inclusive of followers comes from Alan Keith of Genentech who said '_____ is ultimately about creating a way for people to contribute to making something extraordinary happen.'

_____ is one of the most salient aspects of the organizational context. However, defining _____ has been challenging.

   a. Situational leadership
   b. 28-hour day
   c. 1990 Clean Air Act
   d. Leadership

4. Various _____ can be employed dependent on the culture of the business, the nature of the task, the nature of the workforce and the personality and skills of the leaders. This idea was further developed by Robert Tannenbaum and Warren H. Schmidt (1958, 1973) who argued that the style of leadership is dependent upon the prevailing circumstance; therefore leaders should exercise a range of leadership styles and should deploy them as appropriate.

An Autocratic or authoritarian manager makes all the decisions, keeping the information and decision making among the senior management.

Chapter 6. Managing Relationships with Your Bosses, Subordinates, and Peers

a. 28-hour day
b. 1990 Clean Air Act
c. 33 Strategies of War
d. Management styles

5. _____ is a type of thought exhibited by group members who try to minimize conflict and reach consensus without critically testing, analyzing, and evaluating ideas. Individual creativity, uniqueness, and independent thinking are lost in the pursuit of group cohesiveness, as are the advantages of reasonable balance in choice and thought that might normally be obtained by making decisions as a group. During _____, members of the group avoid promoting viewpoints outside the comfort zone of consensus thinking.
   a. Groupthink
   b. Self-report inventory
   c. Psychological statistics
   d. Diffusion of responsibility

6. _____ of the learning curve effect and the closely related experience curve effect express the relationship between equations for experience and efficiency or between efficiency gains and investment in the effort. The experience of 'learning curves' was first observed by the 19th Century German psychologist Hermann Ebbinghaus according to the difficulty of memorizing varying numbers of verbal stimuli, and subsequent learning about the complex processes of learning are discussed in the

The rule used for representing the learning curve effect states that the more times a task has been performed, the less time will be required on each subsequent iteration.

   a. Distribution
   b. Spatial Decision Support Systems
   c. Point biserial correlation coefficient
   d. Models

7. Contingency leadership theory in organizational studies is a type of leadership theory, leadership style, and leadership model that presumes that different leadership styles are contingent to different situations. It is also referred as _____ Â® theory although, as originally convened, the situational theory term is much more restrictive. The original situational theory argues that the best type of leadership is totally determined by the situational variables.Currently there are many styles of leadership.

Chapter 6. Managing Relationships with Your Bosses, Subordinates, and Peers

   a. Situational Leadership
   b. 1990 Clean Air Act
   c. Situational theory
   d. 28-hour day

8. _____ is one of the managerial functions like planning, organizing, staffing and directing. It is an important function because it helps to check the errors and to take the corrective action so that deviation from standards are minimized and stated goals of the organization are achieved in desired manner. According to modern concepts, _____ is a foreseeing action whereas earlier concept of _____ was used only when errors were detected. _____ in management means setting standards, measuring actual performance and taking corrective action.
   a. Control
   b. Decision tree pruning
   c. Schedule of reinforcement
   d. Turnover

9. _____ is an idea in the field of Organizational studies and management which describes the psychology, attitudes, experiences, beliefs and Values (personal and cultural values) of an organization. It has been defined as 'the specific collection of values and norms that are shared by people and groups in an organization and that control the way they interact with each other and with stakeholders outside the organization.'

This definition continues to explain organizational values also known as 'beliefs and ideas about what kinds of goals members of an organization should pursue and ideas about the appropriate kinds or standards of behavior organizational members should use to achieve these goals. From organizational values develop organizational norms, guidelines or expectations that prescribe appropriate kinds of behavior by employees in particular situations and control the behavior of organizational members towards one another.'

_____ is not the same as corporate culture.

   a. Organizational development
   b. Organizational effectiveness
   c. Organizational culture
   d. Union shop

10. _____ refers to increasing the spiritual, political, social or economic strength of individuals and communities. It often involves the empowered developing confidence in their own capacities.

The term Human _____ covers a vast landscape of meanings, interpretations, definitions and disciplines ranging from psychology and philosophy to the highly commercialized Self-Help industry and Motivational sciences.

a. AAAI
b. A Stake in the Outcome
c. A4e
d. Empowerment

11. The _____ captures an expanded spectrum of values and criteria for measuring organizational success: economic, ecological and social. With the ratification of the United Nations and ICLEI _____ standard for urban and community accounting in early 2007, this became the dominant approach to public sector full cost accounting. Similar UN standards apply to natural capital and human capital measurement to assist in measurements required by _____, e.g. the ecoBudget standard for reporting ecological footprint.
   a. Triple bottom line
   b. 1990 Clean Air Act
   c. 28-hour day
   d. 33 Strategies of War

12. _____ is an area of knowledge within organizational theory that studies models and theories about the way an organization learns and adapts.

In Organizational development (OD), learning is a characteristic of an adaptive organization, i.e., an organization that is able to sense changes in signals from its environment (both internal and external) and adapt accordingly.

   a. AAAI
   b. A4e
   c. Organizational learning
   d. A Stake in the Outcome

13. _____ is defined as free choice of one's own acts without external compulsion; and especially as the freedom of the people of a given territory to determine their own political status or independence from their current state. In other words, it is the right of the people of a certain nation to decide how they want to be governed without the influence of any other country. The latter is a complex concept with conflicting definitions and legal criteria for determining which groups may legitimately claim the right to _____..
   a. 1990 Clean Air Act
   b. Populism
   c. 28-hour day
   d. Self-determination

14. _____ is a term originating in military organization theory, but now used more commonly in business management, particularly human resource management. _____ refers to the number of subordinates a supervisor has.

In the hierarchical business organization of the past it was not uncommon to see average spans of 1 to 10 or even less. That is, one manager supervised ten employees on average.

    a. CIFMS
    b. Senior management
    c. Span of control
    d. Mentoring

15. _____ is the study of groups, and also a general term for group processes. Relevant to the fields of psychology, sociology, and communication studies, a group is two or more individuals who are connected to each other by social relationships. Because they interact and influence each other, groups develop a number of dynamic processes that separate them from a random collection of individuals.
    a. Group dynamics
    b. 1990 Clean Air Act
    c. 28-hour day
    d. Collective action

16. A _____ is the formal act of giving up or quitting one's office or position. It can also refer to the act of admitting defeat in a game like chess, indicated by the resigning player declaring 'I resign', turning his king on its side, extending his hand, or stopping the chess clock. A _____ can occur when a person holding a position gained by election or appointment steps down, but leaving a position upon the expiration of a term is not considered _____.
    a. 28-hour day
    b. 1990 Clean Air Act
    c. 33 Strategies of War
    d. Resignation

17. _____ is a contract between two parties, one being the employer and the other being the employee. An employee may be defined as: 'A person in the service of another under any contract of hire, express or implied, oral or written, where the employer has the power or right to control and direct the employee in the material details of how the work is to be performed.' Black's Law Dictionary page 471 (5th ed. 1979.)
    a. Employment counsellor
    b. Exit interview
    c. Employment rate
    d. Employment

Chapter 6. Managing Relationships with Your Bosses, Subordinates, and Peers 31

18. There are two types of _____ relationships: formal and informal. Informal relationships develop on their own between partners. Formal _____, on the other hand, refers to assigned relationships, often associated with organizational _____ programs designed to promote employee development or to assist at-risk children and youth.
    a. Real Property Administrator
    b. Fix it twice
    c. Human resource management system
    d. Mentoring

19. The 'business case for _____', theorizes that in a global marketplace, a company that employs a diverse workforce (both men and women, people of many generations, people from ethnically and racially diverse backgrounds etc.) is better able to understand the demographics of the marketplace it serves and is thus better equipped to thrive in that marketplace than a company that has a more limited range of employee demographics.

    An additional corollary suggests that a company that supports the _____ of its workforce can also improve employee satisfaction, productivity and retention.

    a. Virtual team
    b. Trademark
    c. Diversity
    d. Kanban

20. _____ was a writer, management consultant, and self-described 'social ecologist.' Widely considered to be 'the father of modern management,' his 39 books and countless scholarly and popular articles explored how humans are organized across all sectors of society--in business, government and the nonprofit world. His writings have predicted many of the major developments of the late twentieth century, including privatization and decentralization; the rise of Japan to economic world power; the decisive importance of marketing; and the emergence of the information society with its necessity of lifelong learning. In 1959, Drucker coined the term 'knowledge worker' and later in his life considered knowledge work productivity to be the next frontier of management.
    a. Chrissie Hynde
    b. Debora L. Spar
    c. Jacques Al-Salawat Nasruddin Nasser
    d. Peter Ferdinand Drucker

21. _____ describes how content an individual is with his or her job.

The happier people are within their job, the more satisfied they are said to be. _____ is not the same as motivation, although it is clearly linked.

a. Job analysis
b. Human relations
c. Job satisfaction
d. Goal-setting theory

22. _____ is the pursuit of influencing outcomes -- including public-policy and resource allocation decisions within political, economic, and social systems and institutions -- that directly affect people's current lives. (Cohen, 2001)

Therefore, _____ can be seen as a deliberate process of speaking out on issues of concern in order to exert some influence on behalf of ideas or persons. Based on this definition, Cohen (2001) states that 'ideologues of all persuasions advocate' to bring a change in people's lives.

a. AAAI
b. A4e
c. Advocacy
d. A Stake in the Outcome

23. _____ is a term defined by the Oxford English Dictionary as an individual's 'course or progress through life '. It is usually considered to pertain to remunerative work (and sometimes also formal education.)

The etymology of the term is somewhat ironic in that it comes from the Latin word carrera, which means race .

a. Career planning
b. Spatial mismatch
c. Nursing shortage
d. Career

24. In sociology and social psychology, _____ is the process through which people try to control the impressions other people form of them. It is a goal-directed conscious or unconscious attempt to influence the perceptions of other people about a person, object or event by regulating and controlling information in social interaction. It is usually used synonymously with self-presentation, if a person tries to influence the perception of their image.

a. AAAI
b. A Stake in the Outcome
c. A4e
d. Impression management

Chapter 6. Managing Relationships with Your Bosses, Subordinates, and Peers

25. _____ is communication that expresses something negative about its originator, without this being called for in context by some other person. For example, an admission of guilt is not _____, but emphasis of the extent of one's guilt or an unprompted negative criticism of oneself is.

Self-deprecating humor is humor which relies on the observation of something negative about the person delivering it.

- a. 1990 Clean Air Act
- b. Self-deprecation
- c. 33 Strategies of War
- d. 28-hour day

26. _____ is a concept from the field of social psychology that is commonly used to describe the predisposition that individuals have 'to distort self-appraisals so as to maintain the most favorable self-view'. _____ involves sustaining and augmenting a positive view of the self; specifically, people are likely to over-emphasize favorable evaluations of themselves, while they are inclined to minimize or forget critical assessments of themselves. In addition, the concept of _____ suggests that people tend to look for flattering evaluations from others concerning their achievements and talents.
- a. Self-enhancement
- b. Social loafing
- c. Machiavellianism
- d. Persuasion

Chapter 7. Managing Cultural Diversity

1. The 'business case for _____', theorizes that in a global marketplace, a company that employs a diverse workforce (both men and women, people of many generations, people from ethnically and racially diverse backgrounds etc.) is better able to understand the demographics of the marketplace it serves and is thus better equipped to thrive in that marketplace than a company that has a more limited range of employee demographics.

An additional corollary suggests that a company that supports the _____ of its workforce can also improve employee satisfaction, productivity and retention.

   a. Trademark
   b. Virtual team
   c. Kanban
   d. Diversity

2. _____ refers to an ability to interact effectively with people of different cultures. _____ comprises four components: (a) Awareness of one's own cultural worldview, (b) Attitude towards cultural differences, (c) Knowledge of different cultural practices and worldviews, and (d) cross-cultural skills. Developing _____ results in an ability to understand, communicate with, and effectively interact with people across cultures.
   a. 33 Strategies of War
   b. Cultural competence
   c. 1990 Clean Air Act
   d. 28-hour day

3. _____ or _____ data refers to selected population characteristics as used in government, marketing or opinion research, or the _____ profiles used in such research. Note the distinction from the term 'demography' Commonly-used _____s include race, age, income, disabilities, mobility (in terms of travel time to work or number of vehicles available), educational attainment, home ownership, employment status, and even location.
   a. Abraham Harold Maslow
   b. Adam Smith
   c. Affiliation
   d. Demographic

4. _____ is a term used to describe any moral, political that stresses human interdependence and the importance of a collective, rather than the importance of separate individuals. Collectivists focus on community and society, and seek to give priority to group goals over individual goals. The philosophical underpinnings of _____ are for some related to holism or organicism - the view that the whole is greater than the sum of its parts/pieces.
   a. 1990 Clean Air Act
   b. Collaborative methods
   c. 28-hour day
   d. Collectivism

Chapter 7. Managing Cultural Diversity

5. _____ is a dynamic of being mutually and physically responsible to and sharing a common set of principles with others. This concept differs distinctly from 'dependence' in that an interdependent relationship implies that all participants are emotionally, economically, ecologically and or morally 'interdependent.' Some people advocate freedom or independence as a sort of ultimate good; others do the same with devotion to one's family, community, or society. _____ recognizes the truth in each position and weaves them together.
   a. A Stake in the Outcome
   b. AAAI
   c. A4e
   d. Interdependence

6. _____ describes the situation when output from (or information about the result of) an event or phenomenon in the past will influence the same event/phenomenon in the present or future. When an event is part of a chain of cause-and-effect that forms a circuit or loop, then the event is said to 'feed back' into itself.

   _____ is also a synonym for:

   - _____ signal; the information about the initial event that is the basis for subsequent modification of the event.
   - _____ loop; the causal path that leads from the initial generation of the _____ signal to the subsequent modification of the event.

   _____ is a mechanism, process or signal that is looped back to control a system within itself. Such a loop is called a _____ loop.

   a. Feedback loop
   b. Positive feedback
   c. 1990 Clean Air Act
   d. Feedback

7. _____ consists of the mental process of thinking involved with the process of judging the merits of multiple options and selecting one of them for action. Some simple examples include deciding whether to get up in the morning or go back to sleep, or selecting a given route for a journey. More complex examples (often decisions that affect what a person thinks or their core beliefs) include choosing a lifestyle, religious affiliation, or political position.
   a. Championship mobilization
   b. Trade study
   c. Groups decision making
   d. Choice

8. _____ in its literal sense is the process of transformation of local or regional phenomena into global ones. It can be described as a process by which the people of the world are unified into a single society and function together.

This process is a combination of economic, technological, sociocultural and political forces.

   a. Histogram
   b. Cost Management
   c. Collaborative Planning, Forecasting and Replenishment
   d. Globalization

9. _____ is, in very basic words, a position a firm occupies against its competitors.

According to Michael Porter, the three methods for creating a sustainable _____ are through:

1. Cost leadership

2. Differentiation

3. Focus (economics)

   a. 28-hour day
   b. 1990 Clean Air Act
   c. Theory Z
   d. Competitive advantage

10. _____ is a contract between two parties, one being the employer and the other being the employee. An employee may be defined as: 'A person in the service of another under any contract of hire, express or implied, oral or written, where the employer has the power or right to control and direct the employee in the material details of how the work is to be performed.' Black's Law Dictionary page 471 (5th ed. 1979.)
   a. Employment rate
   b. Employment counsellor
   c. Employment
   d. Exit interview

11. The term _____ was created by President Lyndon B. Johnson when he signed Executive Order 11246 on September 24, 1965, created to prohibit federal contractors from discriminating against employees on the basis of race, sex, creed, religion, color, or national origin. In more recent times, most employers have also added sexual orientation to the list of non-discrimination.

The Executive Order also required contractors to implement affirmative action plans to increase the participation of minorities and women in the workplace.

a. Equal Employment Opportunity
b. AAAI
c. A4e
d. A Stake in the Outcome

12. The U.S. _____ is a federal agency whose goal is ending employment discrimination. The _____ investigates discrimination complaints based on an individual's race, color, national origin, religion, sex, age, disability and retaliation for reporting and/or opposing a discriminatory practice. The Commission is also tasked with filing suits on behalf of alleged victim(s) of discrimination against employers and as an adjudicatory for claims of discrimination brought against federal agencies.
   a. ARCO
   b. Airbus SAS
   c. Equal Employment Opportunity Commission
   d. Airbus Industrie

13. _____s are the recurring expenses which are related to the operation of a business -- or to the operation of a device, component, piece of equipment or facility.

For a commercial enterprise, _____s fall into two broad categories:

- fixed costs, which are the same whether the operation is closed or running at 100% capacity
- variable costs, which may increase depending on whether more production is done, and how it is done (producing 100 items of product might require 10 days of normal time or take 7 days if overtime is used. It may be more or less expensive to use overtime production depending on whether faster production means the product can be more profitable.)

Overhead costs for a business are the cost of resources used by an organization just to maintain its existence. Overhead costs are usually measured in monetary terms, but non-monetary overhead is possible in the form of time required to accomplish tasks.

Examples of overhead costs include:

- payment of rent on the office space a business occupies
- cost of electricity for the office lights
- some office personnel wages

Non-overhead costs are incremental costs, such as the cost of raw materials used in the goods a business sells.

In the case of a device, component, piece of equipment or facility (for the rest of this article, all of these items will be referred to in general as equipment), it is the regular, usual and customary recurring costs of operating the equipment.

Chapter 7. Managing Cultural Diversity

a. Industrial market segmentation
b. Intangible assets
c. Induction programme
d. Operating cost

14. _____ is unwelcome harassment of a sexual nature, or based upon the receiving party's sex or gender. In some contexts or circumstances, _____ may be illegal. It includes a range of behavior from seemingly mild transgressions and annoyances to actual sexual abuse or sexual assault.
   a. 1990 Clean Air Act
   b. Hypernorms
   c. 28-hour day
   d. Sexual harassment

15. In economics, business, retail, and accounting, a _____ is the value of money that has been used up to produce something, and hence is not available for use anymore. In economics, a _____ is an alternative that is given up as a result of a decision. In business, the _____ may be one of acquisition, in which case the amount of money expended to acquire it is counted as _____.
   a. Fixed costs
   b. Cost overrun
   c. Cost allocation
   d. Cost

16. _____ a term coined in the mid-20th century, refers to the belief or attitude that one gender or sex is inferior to, less competent, or less valuable than the other. It can also refer to hatred of, or prejudice towards, either sex as a whole, or the application of stereotypes of masculinity in relation to men, or of femininity in relation to women. It is also called male and female chauvinism.
   a. Reverse discrimination
   b. Separate but equal
   c. 1990 Clean Air Act
   d. Sexism,

17. _____ is the pursuit of influencing outcomes -- including public-policy and resource allocation decisions within political, economic, and social systems and institutions -- that directly affect people's current lives. (Cohen, 2001)

Therefore, _____ can be seen as a deliberate process of speaking out on issues of concern in order to exert some influence on behalf of ideas or persons. Based on this definition, Cohen (2001) states that 'ideologues of all persuasions advocate' to bring a change in people's lives.

a. A Stake in the Outcome
b. Advocacy
c. AAAI
d. A4e

18. The _____, usually abbreviated as NAACP and pronounced N-double-A-C-P, is one of the oldest and most influential civil rights organizations in the United States. Its mission is 'to ensure the political, educational, social, and economic equality of rights of all persons and to eliminate racial hatred and racial discrimination'. Its name, retained in accord with tradition, is one of the last surviving uses of the term colored people.
   a. Prometric
   b. National Association of Corporate Directors
   c. National Association for the Advancement of Colored People
   d. Wells Fargo ' Co.

19. The _____ captures an expanded spectrum of values and criteria for measuring organizational success: economic, ecological and social. With the ratification of the United Nations and ICLEI _____ standard for urban and community accounting in early 2007, this became the dominant approach to public sector full cost accounting. Similar UN standards apply to natural capital and human capital measurement to assist in measurements required by _____, e.g. the ecoBudget standard for reporting ecological footprint.
   a. 33 Strategies of War
   b. 1990 Clean Air Act
   c. 28-hour day
   d. Triple bottom line

20. _____ has been described as the 'process of social influence in which one person can enlist the aid and support of others in the accomplishment of a common task' . A definition more inclusive of followers comes from Alan Keith of Genentech who said '_____ is ultimately about creating a way for people to contribute to making something extraordinary happen.'

_____ is one of the most salient aspects of the organizational context. However, defining _____ has been challenging.

   a. 28-hour day
   b. 1990 Clean Air Act
   c. Situational leadership
   d. Leadership

21. _____ is a type of thought exhibited by group members who try to minimize conflict and reach consensus without critically testing, analyzing, and evaluating ideas. Individual creativity, uniqueness, and independent thinking are lost in the pursuit of group cohesiveness, as are the advantages of reasonable balance in choice and thought that might normally be obtained by making decisions as a group. During _____, members of the group avoid promoting viewpoints outside the comfort zone of consensus thinking.
   a. Groupthink
   b. Self-report inventory
   c. Psychological statistics
   d. Diffusion of responsibility

22. _____ is training for the purpose of increasing participants' cultural awareness, knowledge, and skills, which is based on the assumption that the training will benefit an organization by protecting against civil rights violations, increasing the inclusion of different identity groups, and promoting better teamwork.

_____ has been a controversial issue, due to moral considerations as well as questioned efficiency or even counterproductivity.

According to Michael Bird, many project managers may feel that they are treading new territory as they lead project teams made of individuals from different cultures, heterogeneous mixes, and differing demographics.

   a. Self-disclosure
   b. Soft skill
   c. Role conflict
   d. Diversity training

23. _____ is the term used to describe a situation where different entities cooperate advantageously for a final outcome. Simply defined, it means that the whole is greater than the sum of the individual parts. Although the whole will be greater than each individual part, this is not the concept of _____.
   a. 33 Strategies of War
   b. 28-hour day
   c. 1990 Clean Air Act
   d. Synergy

24. In economics, the term _____ refers to situations where the advancement of a qualified person within the hierarchy of an organization is stopped at a lower level because of some form of discrimination, most commonly sexism or racism, but since the term was coined, '_____' has also come to describe the limited advancement of the deaf, blind, disabled, aged and sexual minorities. It is an unofficial, invisible barrier that prevents women and minorities from advancing in businesses.

This situation is referred to as a 'ceiling' as there is a limitation blocking upward advancement, and 'glass' (transparent) because the limitation is not immediately apparent and is normally an unwritten and unofficial policy. This invisible barrier continues to exist, even though there are no explicit obstacles keeping minorities from acquiring advanced job positions - there are no advertisements that specifically say 'no minorities hired at this establishment', nor are there any formal orders that say 'minorities are not qualified' - but they do lie beneath the surface.

a. 28-hour day
b. 33 Strategies of War
c. 1990 Clean Air Act
d. Glass ceiling

25.

The terms _____ and positive action refer to policies that take race, ethnicity, or gender into consideration in an attempt to promote equal opportunity. The focus of such policies ranges from employment and education to public contracting and health programs. The impetus towards _____ is twofold: to maximize diversity in all levels of society, along with its presumed benefits, and to redress perceived disadvantages due to overt, institutional, or involuntary discrimination.

a. Affiliation
b. Abraham Harold Maslow
c. Adam Smith
d. Affirmative action

26. _____ refers to increasing the spiritual, political, social or economic strength of individuals and communities. It often involves the empowered developing confidence in their own capacities.

The term Human _____ covers a vast landscape of meanings, interpretations, definitions and disciplines ranging from psychology and philosophy to the highly commercialized Self-Help industry and Motivational sciences.

a. A Stake in the Outcome
b. A4e
c. AAAI
d. Empowerment

27. _____ is the equation of personal happiness with consumption and the purchase of material possessions. The term is often associated with criticisms of consumption starting with Thorstein Veblen or, more recently by a movement called Enoughism.

Veblen's subject of examination, the newly emergent middle class arising at the turn of the twentieth century, comes to full fruition by the end of the twentieth century through the process of globalization.

In economics, _____ refers to economic policies placing emphasis on consumption.

   a. Market culture
   b. 28-hour day
   c. 1990 Clean Air Act
   d. Consumerism

28. The _____ is the labour pool in employment. It is generally used to describe those working for a single company or industry, but can also apply to a geographic region like a city, country, state, etc. The term generally excludes the employers or management, and implies those involved in manual labour.
   a. Work-life balance
   b. Pink-collar worker
   c. Division of labour
   d. Workforce

Chapter 8. Creating High-Performing Teams

1. _____ is a civil designation for persons who are incorporated in a fixed or permanent way to a society or group: regular member of the working staff, permanent staff distinguished from a supernumerary.

The term '_____' and its counterpart, 'supernumerary,' originated in Spanish and Latin American academy and government; it is now also used in countries all over the world, such as France, the U.S., England, Italy, etc.

There are _____ members of surgical organizations, of universities, of gastronomical associations, etc.

   a. Adam Smith
   b. Affiliation
   c. Abraham Harold Maslow
   d. Numerary

2. _____ is a concept or doctrine, according to which individuals are to be held responsible for other people's actions by tolerating, ignoring without actively collaborating in these actions.

This concept is found in the Old Testament (or Tanakh), some examples include the account of the Flood, the Tower of Babel, Sodom and Gomorrah and in some interpretations, the Book of Joshua's Achan. In those records entire communities were punished on the act of the vast majority of their members, however it is impossible that there weren't any innocent people, or children too young to be responsible for their deeds.

   a. 28-hour day
   b. Collective responsibility
   c. Self-determination
   d. 1990 Clean Air Act

3. _____ has been described as the 'process of social influence in which one person can enlist the aid and support of others in the accomplishment of a common task' . A definition more inclusive of followers comes from Alan Keith of Genentech who said '_____ is ultimately about creating a way for people to contribute to making something extraordinary happen.'

_____ is one of the most salient aspects of the organizational context. However, defining _____ has been challenging.

   a. 28-hour day
   b. Situational leadership
   c. 1990 Clean Air Act
   d. Leadership

Chapter 8. Creating High-Performing Teams

4. _____ is a type of thought exhibited by group members who try to minimize conflict and reach consensus without critically testing, analyzing, and evaluating ideas. Individual creativity, uniqueness, and independent thinking are lost in the pursuit of group cohesiveness, as are the advantages of reasonable balance in choice and thought that might normally be obtained by making decisions as a group. During _____, members of the group avoid promoting viewpoints outside the comfort zone of consensus thinking.
   a. Groupthink
   b. Diffusion of responsibility
   c. Self-report inventory
   d. Psychological statistics

5. The _____ arose out of the social and intellectual milieu of the 1960s and formed around the concept of cultivating extraordinary potential that its advocates believed to lie largely untapped in most people. The movement took as its premise the belief that through the development of 'human potential', humans can experience an exceptional quality of life filled with happiness, creativity, and fulfillment. As a corollary, those who begin to unleash this assumed potential often find themselves directing their actions within society towards assisting others to release their potential.
   a. 33 Strategies of War
   b. Human Potential Movement
   c. 1990 Clean Air Act
   d. 28-hour day

6. In economics, business, retail, and accounting, a _____ is the value of money that has been used up to produce something, and hence is not available for use anymore. In economics, a _____ is an alternative that is given up as a result of a decision. In business, the _____ may be one of acquisition, in which case the amount of money expended to acquire it is counted as _____.
   a. Cost overrun
   b. Fixed costs
   c. Cost allocation
   d. Cost

7. The _____ assessment is a psychometric questionnaire designed to measure psychological preferences in how people perceive the world and make decisions.[1] These preferences were extrapolated from the typological theories originated by Carl Gustav Jung, as published in his 1921 book Psychological Types. The original developers of the personality inventory were Katharine Cook Briggs and her daughter, Isabel Briggs Myers. They began creating the indicator during World War II, believing that a knowledge of personality preferences would help women who were entering the industrial workforce for the first time identify the sort of war-time jobs where they would be 'most comfortable and effective'.[xiii] The initial questionnaire grew into the _____, which was first published in 1962.

a. 1990 Clean Air Act
b. 33 Strategies of War
c. 28-hour day
d. Myers-Briggs Type Indicator

8. _____ is the study of groups, and also a general term for group processes. Relevant to the fields of psychology, sociology, and communication studies, a group is two or more individuals who are connected to each other by social relationships. Because they interact and influence each other, groups develop a number of dynamic processes that separate them from a random collection of individuals.

a. 28-hour day
b. Collective action
c. 1990 Clean Air Act
d. Group dynamics

9. _____ is an organization's process of defining its strategy and making decisions on allocating its resources to pursue this strategy, including its capital and people. Various business analysis techniques can be used in _____, including SWOT analysis (Strengths, Weaknesses, Opportunities, and Threats) and PEST analysis (Political, Economic, Social, and Technological analysis) or STEER analysis involving Socio-cultural, Technological, Economic, Ecological, and Regulatory factors and EPISTEL (Environment, Political, Informatic, Social, Technological, Economic and Legal)

_____ is the formal consideration of an organization's future course. All _____ deals with at least one of three key questions:

1. 'What do we do?'
2. 'For whom do we do it?'
3. 'How do we excel?'

In business _____, the third question is better phrased 'How can we beat or avoid competition?'. (Bradford and Duncan, page 1.)

a. 28-hour day
b. Strategic planning
c. 33 Strategies of War
d. 1990 Clean Air Act

10. _____ refers to techniques, processes and tools for organizing and coordinating a group of individuals working towards a common goal--i.e. a team.

Several well-known approaches to _____ have come out of academic work. Examples include the Belbin Team Inventory by Meredith Belbin, a method to identify the different types of personalities within teams, and Ken Blanchard's description of 'High Performing Teams'.

   a. Team management
   b. 1990 Clean Air Act
   c. 33 Strategies of War
   d. 28-hour day

11. _____ is the process in which ideas and objects are recognized, differentiated and understood. _____ implies that objects are grouped into categories, usually for some specific purpose. Ideally, a category illuminates a relationship between the subjects and objects of knowledge.
   a. 28-hour day
   b. 1990 Clean Air Act
   c. 33 Strategies of War
   d. Categorization

12. _____ is a dynamic of being mutually and physically responsible to and sharing a common set of principles with others. This concept differs distinctly from 'dependence' in that an interdependent relationship implies that all participants are emotionally, economically, ecologically and or morally 'interdependent.' Some people advocate freedom or independence as a sort of ultimate good; others do the same with devotion to one's family, community, or society. _____ recognizes the truth in each position and weaves them together.
   a. A Stake in the Outcome
   b. AAAI
   c. A4e
   d. Interdependence

13. The _____ captures an expanded spectrum of values and criteria for measuring organizational success: economic, ecological and social. With the ratification of the United Nations and ICLEI _____ standard for urban and community accounting in early 2007, this became the dominant approach to public sector full cost accounting. Similar UN standards apply to natural capital and human capital measurement to assist in measurements required by _____, e.g. the ecoBudget standard for reporting ecological footprint.
   a. 33 Strategies of War
   b. 28-hour day
   c. 1990 Clean Air Act
   d. Triple bottom line

Chapter 8. Creating High-Performing Teams

14. The goal of most research on _____ is to learn why and how small groups change over time. To do this, researchers examine patterns of change and continuity in groups over time. Aspects of a group that might be studied include the quality of the output produced by a group, the type and frequency of its activities, its cohesiveness, the existence of conflict, etc.
    a. 28-hour day
    b. 1990 Clean Air Act
    c. 33 Strategies of War
    d. Group development

15. _____ is the term used to describe a situation where different entities cooperate advantageously for a final outcome. Simply defined, it means that the whole is greater than the sum of the individual parts. Although the whole will be greater than each individual part, this is not the concept of _____.
    a. 1990 Clean Air Act
    b. 28-hour day
    c. 33 Strategies of War
    d. Synergy

16. A _____ is defined as someone who controls access to something. It also refers to individuals who decide whether a given message will be distributed by a mass medium.

    _____s serve several different purposes such as academic admissions, financial advising, and news editing.

    a. 33 Strategies of War
    b. 28-hour day
    c. Gatekeeper
    d. 1990 Clean Air Act

Chapter 9. Diverse Teams and Virtual Teams: Managing Differences and Distances

1. _____ refers to techniques, processes and tools for organizing and coordinating a group of individuals working towards a common goal--i.e. a team.

Several well-known approaches to _____ have come out of academic work. Examples include the Belbin Team Inventory by Meredith Belbin, a method to identify the different types of personalities within teams, and Ken Blanchard's description of 'High Performing Teams'.

  a. Team management
  b. 33 Strategies of War
  c. 1990 Clean Air Act
  d. 28-hour day

2. _____ is a civil designation for persons who are incorporated in a fixed or permanent way to a society or group: regular member of the working staff, permanent staff distinguished from a supernumerary.

The term '_____' and its counterpart, 'supernumerary,' originated in Spanish and Latin American academy and government; it is now also used in countries all over the world, such as France, the U.S., England, Italy, etc.

There are _____ members of surgical organizations, of universities, of gastronomical associations, etc.

  a. Affiliation
  b. Abraham Harold Maslow
  c. Numerary
  d. Adam Smith

3. The 'business case for _____', theorizes that in a global marketplace, a company that employs a diverse workforce (both men and women, people of many generations, people from ethnically and racially diverse backgrounds etc.) is better able to understand the demographics of the marketplace it serves and is thus better equipped to thrive in that marketplace than a company that has a more limited range of employee demographics.

An additional corollary suggests that a company that supports the _____ of its workforce can also improve employee satisfaction, productivity and retention.

  a. Trademark
  b. Diversity
  c. Kanban
  d. Virtual team

Chapter 9. Diverse Teams and Virtual Teams: Managing Differences and Distances

4. _____ is the study of groups, and also a general term for group processes. Relevant to the fields of psychology, sociology, and communication studies, a group is two or more individuals who are connected to each other by social relationships. Because they interact and influence each other, groups develop a number of dynamic processes that separate them from a random collection of individuals.
    a. 1990 Clean Air Act
    b. Collective action
    c. 28-hour day
    d. Group dynamics

5. In sociology, _____ is the social process of becoming or being made marginal (to relegate or confine to a lower social standing or outer limit or edge, as of social standing); 'the _____ of the underclass'; '_____ of literature' and many other are some examples. _____ involves people being denied degrees of power. _____ has the potential to result in severe material deprivation, and in its most extreme form can exterminate groups.
    a. Role conflict
    b. Social network analysis
    c. Marginalization
    d. Soft skill

6. In probability theory, a probability distribution is called _____ if its cumulative distribution function is _____. This is equivalent to saying that for random variables X with the distribution in question, Pr[X = a] = 0 for all real numbers a, i.e.: the probability that X attains the value a is zero, for any number a. If the distribution of X is _____ then X is called a _____ random variable.
    a. Decision tree pruning
    b. Pay Band
    c. Connectionist expert systems
    d. Continuous

7. _____ is a management process whereby delivery (customer valued) processes are constantly evaluated and improved in the light of their efficiency, effectiveness and flexibility.

Some see it as a meta process for most management systems (Business Process Management, Quality Management, Project Management). Deming saw it as part of the 'system' whereby feedback from the process and customer were evaluated against organisational goals.

    a. Critical Success Factor
    b. Continuous Improvement Process
    c. Sole proprietorship
    d. First-mover advantage

Chapter 9. Diverse Teams and Virtual Teams: Managing Differences and Distances

8. _____ has been described as the 'process of social influence in which one person can enlist the aid and support of others in the accomplishment of a common task'. A definition more inclusive of followers comes from Alan Keith of Genentech who said '_____ is ultimately about creating a way for people to contribute to making something extraordinary happen.'

_____ is one of the most salient aspects of the organizational context. However, defining _____ has been challenging.

   a. 28-hour day
   b. Situational leadership
   c. 1990 Clean Air Act
   d. Leadership

9. _____ is a type of thought exhibited by group members who try to minimize conflict and reach consensus without critically testing, analyzing, and evaluating ideas. Individual creativity, uniqueness, and independent thinking are lost in the pursuit of group cohesiveness, as are the advantages of reasonable balance in choice and thought that might normally be obtained by making decisions as a group. During _____, members of the group avoid promoting viewpoints outside the comfort zone of consensus thinking.
   a. Psychological statistics
   b. Groupthink
   c. Self-report inventory
   d. Diffusion of responsibility

10. _____ is an idea in the field of Organizational studies and management which describes the psychology, attitudes, experiences, beliefs and Values (personal and cultural values) of an organization. It has been defined as 'the specific collection of values and norms that are shared by people and groups in an organization and that control the way they interact with each other and with stakeholders outside the organization.'

This definition continues to explain organizational values also known as 'beliefs and ideas about what kinds of goals members of an organization should pursue and ideas about the appropriate kinds or standards of behavior organizational members should use to achieve these goals. From organizational values develop organizational norms, guidelines or expectations that prescribe appropriate kinds of behavior by employees in particular situations and control the behavior of organizational members towards one another.'

_____ is not the same as corporate culture.

   a. Organizational development
   b. Organizational culture
   c. Organizational effectiveness
   d. Union shop

Chapter 9. Diverse Teams and Virtual Teams: Managing Differences and Distances

11. _____ is a dynamic of being mutually and physically responsible to and sharing a common set of principles with others. This concept differs distinctly from 'dependence' in that an interdependent relationship implies that all participants are emotionally, economically, ecologically and or morally 'interdependent.' Some people advocate freedom or independence as a sort of ultimate good; others do the same with devotion to one's family, community, or society. _____ recognizes the truth in each position and weaves them together.
   a. Interdependence
   b. AAAI
   c. A Stake in the Outcome
   d. A4e

12. A _____ -- also known as a geographically dispersed team -- is a group of individuals who work across time, space, and organizational boundaries with links strengthened by webs of communication technology. They have complementary skills and are committed to a common purpose, have interdependent performance goals, and share an approach to work for which they hold themselves mutually accountable. Geographically dispersed teams allow organizations to hire and retain the best people regardless of location.
   a. Risk management
   b. Virtual team
   c. Trademark
   d. Kanban

13. The term '_____' refers to the concept of collecting information and attempting to spot a pattern in the information. In some fields of study, the term '_____' has more formally-defined meanings.

In project management _____ is a mathematical technique that uses historical results to predict future outcome.

   a. Trend analysis
   b. Stepwise regression
   c. Least squares
   d. Regression analysis

14. A _____ is a professional who provides advice in a particular area of expertise such as management, accountancy, the environment, entertainment, technology, law , human resources, marketing, medicine, finance, economics, public affairs, communication, engineering, sound system design, graphic design, or waste management.

A _____ is usually an expert or a professional in a specific field and has a wide knowledge of the subject matter. A _____ usually works for a consultancy firm or is self-employed, and engages with multiple and changing clients.

a. 1990 Clean Air Act
b. 33 Strategies of War
c. Consultant
d. 28-hour day

15. _____ in its literal sense is the process of transformation of local or regional phenomena into global ones. It can be described as a process by which the people of the world are unified into a single society and function together.

This process is a combination of economic, technological, sociocultural and political forces.

a. Collaborative Planning, Forecasting and Replenishment
b. Histogram
c. Cost Management
d. Globalization

16. _____ occurs when an individual's thoughts or actions are affected by other people. _____ takes many forms and can be seen in conformity, socialization, peer pressure, obedience, leadership, persuasion, sales, and marketing. Harvard psychologist, Herbert Kelman identified three broad varieties of _____.
a. Social awareness
b. Social influence
c. Role conflict
d. Soft skill

17. In economics, business, retail, and accounting, a _____ is the value of money that has been used up to produce something, and hence is not available for use anymore. In economics, a _____ is an alternative that is given up as a result of a decision. In business, the _____ may be one of acquisition, in which case the amount of money expended to acquire it is counted as _____.
a. Cost allocation
b. Cost overrun
c. Cost
d. Fixed costs

Chapter 10. Crafting a Life

1. _____ is a broad concept including proper prioritizing between career and ambition on one hand, compared with pleasure, leisure, family and spiritual development on the other.

As the separation between work and home life has diminished, this concept has become more relevant than ever before.

The expression was first used in the late 1970s to describe the balance between an individual's work and personal life.

   a. Division of labour
   b. Workforce
   c. Work-life balance
   d. Quality of working life

2. In psychology, _____ reflects a person's overall evaluation or appraisal of his or her own worth.

   _____ encompasses beliefs (for example, 'I am competent/incompetent') and emotions (for example, triumph/despair, pride/shame.) Behavior may reflect _____

   a. 1990 Clean Air Act
   b. 33 Strategies of War
   c. 28-hour day
   d. Self-esteem

3. The 'business case for _____', theorizes that in a global marketplace, a company that employs a diverse workforce (both men and women, people of many generations, people from ethnically and racially diverse backgrounds etc.) is better able to understand the demographics of the marketplace it serves and is thus better equipped to thrive in that marketplace than a company that has a more limited range of employee demographics.

An additional corollary suggests that a company that supports the _____ of its workforce can also improve employee satisfaction, productivity and retention.

   a. Virtual team
   b. Trademark
   c. Kanban
   d. Diversity

4. People often hold beliefs about themselves, the world, and the future which are more positive than reality can sustain. These beliefs are called _____s.

Three types of _____s have been documented: self-aggrandizing self-perceptions (the above-average effect, where people consistently regard themselves more positively and less negatively than they regard others, and than others regard them), perceptions of mastery (where most people believe that they can exert more personal control over environmental circumstances than is actually the case), and unrealistic 'optimism' (deontology) (optimism bias, where people are optimistic and believe that the present is better than the past, and the future will be better than the present.)

a. 33 Strategies of War
b. 1990 Clean Air Act
c. 28-hour day
d. Positive illusion

5. _____ has been described as the 'process of social influence in which one person can enlist the aid and support of others in the accomplishment of a common task' . A definition more inclusive of followers comes from Alan Keith of Genentech who said '_____ is ultimately about creating a way for people to contribute to making something extraordinary happen.'

_____ is one of the most salient aspects of the organizational context. However, defining _____ has been challenging.

a. Leadership
b. Situational leadership
c. 1990 Clean Air Act
d. 28-hour day

6. _____ is a type of thought exhibited by group members who try to minimize conflict and reach consensus without critically testing, analyzing, and evaluating ideas. Individual creativity, uniqueness, and independent thinking are lost in the pursuit of group cohesiveness, as are the advantages of reasonable balance in choice and thought that might normally be obtained by making decisions as a group. During _____, members of the group avoid promoting viewpoints outside the comfort zone of consensus thinking.

a. Psychological statistics
b. Diffusion of responsibility
c. Self-report inventory
d. Groupthink

7. _____ or _____ data refers to selected population characteristics as used in government, marketing or opinion research, or the _____ profiles used in such research. Note the distinction from the term 'demography' Commonly-used _____s include race, age, income, disabilities, mobility (in terms of travel time to work or number of vehicles available), educational attainment, home ownership, employment status, and even location.

a. Adam Smith
b. Abraham Harold Maslow
c. Affiliation
d. Demographic

8. The _____ is the labour pool in employment. It is generally used to describe those working for a single company or industry, but can also apply to a geographic region like a city, country, state, etc. The term generally excludes the employers or management, and implies those involved in manual labour.
   a. Division of labour
   b. Work-life balance
   c. Pink-collar worker
   d. Workforce

9. _____ refers to increasing the spiritual, political, social or economic strength of individuals and communities. It often involves the empowered developing confidence in their own capacities.

The term Human _____ covers a vast landscape of meanings, interpretations, definitions and disciplines ranging from psychology and philosophy to the highly commercialized Self-Help industry and Motivational sciences.

   a. A Stake in the Outcome
   b. AAAI
   c. A4e
   d. Empowerment

10. The _____ of 1996 (PRWORA, Pub.L. 104-193, 110 Stat. 2105, enacted August 22, 1996) is a United States federal law considered to be a fundamental shift in both the method and goal of federal cash assistance to the poor.
    a. Reporting of Injuries, Diseases and Dangerous Occurrences Regulations
    b. Personal Responsibility and Work Opportunity Reconciliation Act
    c. Reverification
    d. Design patent

11. _____ is a term defined by the Oxford English Dictionary as an individual's 'course or progress through life '. It is usually considered to pertain to remunerative work (and sometimes also formal education.)

The etymology of the term is somewhat ironic in that it comes from the Latin word carrera, which means race .

a. Spatial mismatch
b. Career
c. Career planning
d. Nursing shortage

12. _____, e-commuting, e-work, telework, working from home (WFH), or working at home (WAH) is a work arrangement in which employees enjoy flexibility in working location and hours. In other words, the daily commute to a central place of work is replaced by telecommunication links. Many work from home, while others, occasionally also referred to as nomad workers or web commuters utilize mobile telecommunications technology to work from coffee shops or myriad other locations.
   a. 28-hour day
   b. 1990 Clean Air Act
   c. 33 Strategies of War
   d. Telecommuting

13. _____ is a field of study in neuroscience and psychology focusing on a child's development in terms of information processing, conceptual resources, perceptual skill, and other topics in cognitive psychology. A large portion of research has gone into understanding how a child conceptualizes the world. Jean Piaget was a major force in the founding of this field, forming his 'theory of _____'.
   a. 33 Strategies of War
   b. Cognitive development
   c. 28-hour day
   d. 1990 Clean Air Act

14. _____ consists of the mental process of thinking involved with the process of judging the merits of multiple options and selecting one of them for action. Some simple examples include deciding whether to get up in the morning or go back to sleep, or selecting a given route for a journey. More complex examples (often decisions that affect what a person thinks or their core beliefs) include choosing a lifestyle, religious affiliation, or political position.
   a. Championship mobilization
   b. Trade study
   c. Groups decision making
   d. Choice

15. _____ is the experience that a person has working, or working in a specific field or occupation.

The phrase is sometimes used to mean a type of volunteer work that is commonly intended for young people -- often students -- to get a feel for professional working environments. This usage is common in the United Kingdom, while the American equivalent is intern.

a. Job fair
b. Work experience
c. TDY
d. Career break

ANSWER KEY

Chapter 1
1. c   2. b   3. d   4. d   5. d   6. d   7. d   8. d   9. d   10. d
11. d   12. d   13. d   14. a   15. b   16. d   17. c   18. a

Chapter 2
1. d   2. d   3. d   4. a   5. d   6. a   7. a   8. d   9. d   10. d
11. a   12. d   13. c   14. b   15. d   16. b   17. d

Chapter 3
1. a   2. c   3. d   4. a   5. d   6. d   7. d   8. d

Chapter 4
1. d   2. d   3. c   4. d   5. d   6. d   7. c   8. c   9. d   10. a
11. b   12. d   13. b   14. d

Chapter 5
1. b   2. c   3. d   4. c   5. d   6. c   7. a   8. d   9. b   10. d
11. a   12. a   13. d   14. a   15. d

Chapter 6
1. d   2. d   3. d   4. d   5. a   6. d   7. a   8. a   9. c   10. d
11. a   12. c   13. d   14. c   15. a   16. d   17. d   18. d   19. c   20. d
21. c   22. c   23. d   24. d   25. b   26. a

Chapter 7
1. d   2. b   3. d   4. d   5. d   6. d   7. d   8. d   9. d   10. c
11. a   12. c   13. d   14. d   15. d   16. d   17. b   18. c   19. d   20. d
21. a   22. d   23. d   24. d   25. d   26. d   27. d   28. d

Chapter 8
1. d   2. b   3. d   4. a   5. b   6. d   7. d   8. d   9. b   10. a
11. d   12. d   13. d   14. d   15. d   16. c

Chapter 9
1. a   2. c   3. b   4. d   5. c   6. d   7. b   8. d   9. b   10. b
11. a   12. b   13. a   14. c   15. d   16. b   17. c

Chapter 10
1. c   2. d   3. d   4. d   5. a   6. d   7. d   8. d   9. d   10. b
11. b   12. d   13. b   14. d   15. b

www.ingramcontent.com/pod-product-compliance
Lightning Source LLC
Chambersburg PA
CBHW080743250426
43671CB00038B/2854